112 WAYS FOR KIDS TO HAVE FUN WITHOUT MONEY

Matthew

To

Be inspired to have Fun!

Sam Gross

Written by Sam Gross
with Kate Gross
Illustrated by Greg Rockwell

FERNE PRESS

112 Ways for Kids to Have Fun without Money
Copyright © 2013 by Sam Gross with Kate Gross

Illustrations created by Greg Rockwell
Illustrations created with pen and ink
Layout and cover design by Susan Leonard

Printed in the United States of America

Summary: 112 ways to entertain kids without using money.

Library of Congress Cataloging-in-Publication Data
Gross, Sam with Kate Gross
112 Ways for Kids to Have Fun without Money/Sam Gross with Kate
Gross–First Edition
ISBN-13: 978-1-938326-11-0
1. Juvenile Non-fiction. 2. Fun things to do without money. 3. Family
and friends.
I. Gross, Sam II. Title
Library of Congress Control Number: 2013930193

FERNE PRESS

Ferne Press is an imprint of Nelson Publishing & Marketing
366 Welch Road, Northville, MI 48167
www.nelsonpublishingandmarketing.com
(248) 735-0418

This book is dedicated to Mrs. Londrigan, my computer teacher and the person who assigned the topic in the first place; and to all my friends who were really supportive of me as I was getting it published; to my Nama, who thought the book was a good idea and showed it to the publisher.

Also to Owen, my brother, who I've done about eighty percent of these things with, and finally to my mom, who helped me make better sense of my ideas.

Enjoy these 112 ways to have fun
without money, and afterward, why
not make your own list? ☺

1.

Practice yo-yo tricks.

2.

Blow bubbles at your cat
or dog. If she tries to catch
them, run, and see if she'll
chase the bubbles.

3.

Make a playing
card castle.

4.

Identify things, like different birds, leaves, or bugs you find.

5.

Dig to China, or at least as far down as you can, with permission of course!

6.

Walk around your house. Do it again while looking straight up.

7.

Make friendship bracelets and stack them up your arm. There are so many different ways to make bracelets and so many different types of material, like string, rubber bands, nylon cords, and yarn. Part of the fun is to check out a book at the library or look up directions on the Internet. There are lots of websites that kids can use for directions that show up on a "Google" search.

8.

Make up a funny story with a friend about random things.

9.

Listen to a story that someone else reads.

10.

Play "I Spy" with someone.

11.

Make up your own kingdom. Create a banner for it. Decide who is going to be the knight, king, horse, queen, etc., and then go on missions to do fun stuff.

12.

Play football with your family. Play flag football using bandannas for flags.

13.

Set up an Olympic course of real and crazy made-up games in your backyard. Challenge each other for the best time or practice it yourself.

14.

Make an obstacle course out of things you have in your backyard. Time yourself doing the course. List the times to find your fastest.

15.

Decorate your bike helmet with any stickers or pipe cleaners that you have.

16.

Practice your favorite sport.

17.

Run through the sprinkler. Play Reverse Limbo. Turn the water low and try to jump over it. Keep turning the water up to see how high you can make it over the sprinkler.

18.

Blend your own smoothie creations. Try using different fruits and juices each time and have a tasting to see which flavor people at your house like best.

19.

Watch yourself try to eat a lemon in the mirror.

20.

Try a new food.

21.

Investigate how something is made on the computer. Start with methane.

22.

Make a clay volcano. Pour in baking soda and vinegar and watch it explode! This is the type of experiment where trial and error can be more fun than being told exactly how to do it. Experiment with different amounts of baking soda and vinegar to see what combinations make the biggest eruption. You can practice in a tall glass or beaker with small amounts before loading up the clay volcano. You can use red and orange food dye in the final mixture to really make the eruption look like lava.

23.

Play PIG with your mom and dad. See the Appendix for directions.

24.

Play hockey with your dad. Use a broom and a ball if you don't have hockey gear.

25.

Ask a grandparent to teach you something that they like to do, like fly RC planes, knit, golf, or play a game.

26.

Make a backyard camp with tents and cozy blankets. Read stories, catch fireflies or other bugs to watch in a jar, and have snacks with your siblings or friends.

27.

Take a hike up the tallest hill you can find, and then run down while yelling like a screaming maniac.

28.

Play tag, change the rules, and play it again.

29.

Take a _____ walk, and tally up all the _____ you see. Make it anything you like: robins, green cars, rabbits, whatever!

30.

Borrow a bird book. Keep a list of all of the birds that you see.

31.

Play "Follow the Leader" through a park. Take turns being the leader.

32.

Make paper airplanes and play airplane golf by throwing the airplanes toward a target. Write down how many throws it takes each person to hit each target. Lowest score wins. Bird houses and hula hoops hanging from trees make great targets.

33.

Have a foam dart gun war if you have some.

34.

See who can throw a football the farthest, you or your friend. Congratulate the winner, even if it's not you.

35.

Build a snow fort. Make sure it has high enough walls to hide behind by digging the snow out of your fort so that the ground is the floor. Make snowballs. Store them in a secret compartment in the fort. Invite a friend for a snowball fight.

36.

If it snows a lot, go outside and measure where it's deepest. Use a ruler to measure the depth and record it in a notebook. Measure straight down in many different places in your yard. Record the measurements and "report" your findings to your family.

37.

Bake cupcakes and have a sale in your front yard. Give the money to your favorite charity.

38.

Bake a cake with an adult.

39.

Make some lemonade and have a lemonade stand with a friend.

40.

Classify things in your room, like books or toys.

41.

Take a bubble bath. Make crazy bubble beards and use the bubbles to style your hair in funny ways.

42.

Make your bed a new way; change the stuffed animals that you have on it.

43.

Draw your own pictures to make a memory game to play with someone younger.

44.

Learn to shuffle playing cards.

45.

Get a drink of water, count the sips you can take before you take a breath.

46.

Play hide-and-seek.

47.

Build with wooden or plastic blocks.

48.

Play dodge bowling ball (this is a joke!). Use action figures or build Lego towers for bowling pins and bowl with a soft ball in the house.

49.

Choose a board game you are tired of playing, change all the rules, and play it a new way. Or, combine a couple of board games to make a new game.

50.

Build a pillow and blanket fort. Defend your fort!

51.

Plan a "favorites" night. The object of the night is to have a family dinner where each person picks one favorite item to be part of the menu and then the conversation at the dinner table is all about "favorites." It starts by having each member of the family pick one "favorite" for the menu. Let one person pick the main course. Others can pick the side dishes, drinks, and maybe even dessert. It can be funny to end up with foods that might not normally go together. During the meal, each person will take turns asking everyone to give their answer to questions about their favorites, such as favorite book, movie, game, sport, color, animal, etc.

52.

Wash the dishes, and then blow the bubbles around the sink with a straw.

53.

Make a list of your relatives. Sort by people with the same names or write them in alphabetical order.

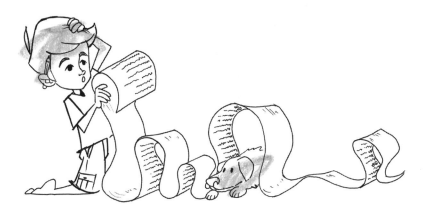

54.

Make cards for your family to send to friends or relatives on holidays during the year.

55.

Write a letter to a faraway relative.

56.

Make a treasure hunt. Hide a toy or something you don't want for your treasure. Make a map to find it and give it to someone to solve, or trade maps with someone and see who finds the treasure first.

57.

Make origami creations. Look up designs online if you don't have a book.

58.

Zing a rubber band with a friend. Measure the distances to see whose went the farthest.

59.

Set up trick-or-treating in the middle of July. Dress up with your neighbors and have fun!

60.

Celebrate your birthday on a different day.

61.

Plan a party for someone for no particular reason. Hang streamers and balloons, make a cake, and then tell the person all the reasons why they are special to you.

62.

Go to the bathroom. Stay in and yell
"OCCUPIED!"

63.

Build your own creation with Legos.

64.

Write some riddles. Challenge a friend to solve
them.

65.

Call your grandparents and tell them about something going on in your neighborhood or in your classroom.

66.

Build a puzzle alone, with a friend, or with your family.

67.

Help a senior citizen. Call the senior center in your town for ideas. Take some of your artwork to a nursing home to show to some of the patients. Tell them how you made it.

68.

Make your own zoo. Use toy animals or stuffed animals. Design their enclosures and then make fact cards for each exhibit.

69.

Check out free museum passes from the library. Go to the zoo, read the animal facts, and write down the ten that most surprised you.

70.

Point to a place on a map without looking, see what it is, and then look up facts about it.

71.

Play "What am I?" Think of an animal and give clues about it. Have your family members guess what you are. "I have sticky feet so I can crawl up walls, live in warm areas, and I am a reptile. What am I?" The correct guesser goes next.

72.

Volunteer to walk a neighbor's dog (if it is friendly).

73.

Give a pet some love. Play with it, brush it, or teach it a new trick.

74.

Make your own soda by mixing club soda and juice.

75.

Burp really loudly.

76.

Bake a pie with a grown-up. Try making fun shapes with the top crust.

77.

Write your own book.

78.

Make sentences with magnet words or letters on the fridge.

79.

Write and illustrate your own comic strip.

80.

Make your own Halloween costume, or one to wear just for fun. Use old clothes or pieces of fabric to create a mummy, scarecrow, rapper, or whatever you like.

81.

Make a haunted house and invite your friends to come through it.

82.

Start a collection, like rocks, stamps, or coins. Research the items in your collection on the Internet or at the library.

83.

Design a car in your head. Try to make blueprints for it. Include lots of cool features and gadgets. Mail the blueprint to someone else who likes cars and remember to ask them to send back their comments.

84.

Make a Lego army out of mini-figures you create. Stage a battle between the troops.

85.

Read a book, and then write a review online.

86.

Go to the library and pick out a book that you think looks interesting. Pick a book for someone younger than you, such as a sibling or a neighbor, and read it to them.

87.

Read a family magazine at the library to get ideas for fun treats to make for a holiday, like apple vampire mouths for Halloween. See Appendix for directions.

88.

Set a family record for running up the stairs in shoes the fastest. Try it again barefoot.

89.

Ride a scooter. Create a "Scooter Training School" for a friend or sibling.

90.

Talk to your neighbors (the grown-up ones you know).

91.

Make up silly missions that have to be accomplished before bedtime. Write up the missions in the morning with the directions that no one goes to bed until they have skipped everywhere instead of walked, or until they have worn a paper moustache through dinner.

92.

Plan a family meal. Make a grocery list of all the ingredients. When you go to the store, see how many of the things you can find by yourself. Make a list of conversation ideas to use while eating.

93.

Make up a new game during recess or play one we made up called Hooper-inner. See Appendix for instructions.

94.

Build a tree house.

95.

Dance to your favorite song.

96.

Watch the Olympics.

97.

Play "Cash Cab" while on a drive. One person reads questions from a trivia book. The others answer. Start with penny questions, then nickel questions, and finally dime questions. You get three wrong answers before you're out and can do a "phone a friend" for one question.

98.

Paint your toenails in a pattern of colors.

99.

Watch and then try to copy your favorite singer's dance moves.

100.

Watch a new TV show and tell a friend if you like it.

101.

Check out a book of card games from the library. Teach yourself a different version of solitaire.

102.

Challenge a grown-up to a bear crawl race down the driveway. The winner picks the next kind of race.

103.

Bake and decorate sugar cookies.

104.

Make up a song about a younger sibling's or a friend's favorite stuffed animal or blanket to the tune of "Mary Had a Little Lamb." Sing it with him or her.

105.

Play math flashcard war.

106.

Sing or write your own new song.

107.

Use a map to play "I Spy" to find countries. Try using different map clues each time, like the color of the country or the features it has (like mountains, shape, and coordinates).

108.

Check off your favorite activities in this book.

109.

Find a friend at church. Talk to them after the service.

110.

Make up your own list of ways to make you or someone else happy.

111.

Think about what the world would look like if people had never existed. Draw or paint a picture of what you imagined.

112.

Plan tomorrow.

Before you share this book with a friend, go back and look for the hidden initials (SG & GR) in each illustration.

APPENDIX

PIG (#23): This is a shorter version of the basketball game called "HORSE." The object of the game is to make shots with a basketball that other players cannot. Players take turns shooting a basketball at a hoop. When a player makes a basket, all other players must shoot from the exact same spot to try to make a basket. If a player misses the shot, they get a letter from the word "PIG." The first missed shot is the "P," the second is the "I," and the final missed shot is the "G." When a player gets all three letters, they are out of the game. The object is to be the last player left.

Players continue to take turns trying new shots from new locations while all other players follow and try to make the same exact shot. Players must copy the place and style of the shot: a layup, jump-shot, free throw, etc. It is really fun to try silly shots, like standing on one leg or shooting with your eyes closed. PIG can be played with any number of players, but the more players you have, the longer it takes. If you have really young players, they can use a shorter hoop or even a bucket instead of an actual basketball hoop.

APPLE VAMPIRE MOUTHS (#87): Quarter an apple and scoop out the core. On the skin side, cut out a mouth-shaped wedge so that the red skin of the apple looks like a top and bottom lip. Use slivered almonds or white chocolate chips as the vampire fangs. Use peanut butter to "glue" the fangs to the top and bottom. It also makes a yummy snack.

HOOPER-INNER (#93): It is played with at least three people. One, two, or three are IT depending on how many people you have. They hold hula-hoops in front of themselves and chase the other people trying to put the hoops over their heads. Make up safe spots for the people who are not IT. If you get a hoop over your head, you have to pick up the hoop and be IT. You can't throw a hoop onto someone. There are no winners; you just play until you get bored. It is just like tag, but instead of tagging, you put the hoop over their heads.

Dear Readers, Teachers, and Families,

This book began as a third-grade computer class assignment. It has come a long way since Sam's grandma read it and thought it would make a good book. Sam spent a lot of time clarifying ideas and changing it into more of a how-to book. Warning: parts may make you laugh!

Like most everyone, we have gone through times of feeling more pinched for money and times when the budget is easier. Throughout, we have tried to teach our boys that no amount of money can buy your happiness; happiness comes from within. It sounds easy until you try to rationalize to a little one why one more toy won't make the difference in their life! I find myself saying to them, "Find your happy!" It is a choice to be happy in any situation.

Now, kids cannot always find their own happiness and that is how this book came to be. It is a collection of ideas Sam came up with, things he has done with his brothers, and activities we have done together as a family as a way of finding fun and happiness without spending much money. We hope it provides inspiration to families on days when they need a boost of ideas. We believe that once you start doing some of these activities, your family will come up with even more on their own.

As a teacher, I know that there are many classroom applications for this book. Beyond doing activities from the book in class or in an outdoor lesson, children can be encouraged to dream up their own lists, to plan tomorrow.

We hope you enjoy it as much as we have enjoyed creating it!

Kate and Sam Gross

ABOUT THE AUTHOR

Photo credit: Zdenka Leonard, ZD photography

Sam is eleven years old and lives with his mom, dad, and three little brothers, Owen, Will, and Bryce, in Flushing, Michigan. He has a cat named Mischief and a dog named Tigerlily. He really likes football, swimming, basketball, and reading. Sam is thankful for his many good friends at home and at school who treat him so well. Sam is a big fan of the Olympics and the Ohio State Buckeyes—try not to hold that against him!

For more information about Sam, please visit www.samgrossbooks.com.

ABOUT THE ILLUSTRATOR

Greg Rockwell was born and still lives in Flint, Michigan. He has loved drawing since he could hold a pencil. "112 Ways for Kids to Have Fun without Money" is his first illustration project. He is currently in college studying animation to pursue a career in art.